To Richa

Best wi

new role.

Jeremy.

To Ros and all my family,
especially Anneliese and Margaret
- the new generation.

Second edition 2020

First published 2017

Squawk Publishing

© Jeremy Rudd, 2017

The right of Jeremy Rudd to be identified as the Author of this work has been asserted in accordance with the Copyright, Designs and Patents Act 1988.

British Library Cataloguing in Publication Data.
A catalogue record for this book is available from the British Library.

ISBN 978-1-9998694-2-7

It is a true gift to be able to explain complex ideas simply and clearly and in this book Jeremy does just that. I would recommend '4 Magic Steps' to all management teams and would encourage a re-read on an annual basis. Too often the intricacies of any business conceal the prime objective and distract management. This book reminds us exactly what our priorities should be.

Ted Smith is Operating Partner, and Chairman of G Square's Healthcare Advisory Board, Chairman of Accomplish Group, Keys Group, Pharmacy2U and Dental Care Group

I was reviewing business books and had just finished one about the destiny of business using complex terminology such as theory of computability, theorem of transaction costs and finally the law of the distributed ledger - phew I thought I needed a PHD to understand it! Thankfully I then picked up Jeremy's '4 Magic Steps' it is a breath of fresh air, a simple, readable and enlightening story that is a user guide for startup and established enterprises that will help anyone develop, analyze and adapt their current business plan to be financially viable.

Jerry Peterson, Florida, former CEO & Chairman of UK and US companies.

'This new book is excellent. It certainly makes a refreshing change from reading tedious business books that are often less accessible and much less well explained! It's a fantastic primer for new entrepreneurs, and for top management of businesses who have never had a formal business education and so often fall into the usual traps like losing touch with your customers, under-pricing, overtrading / working capital shortage, and not keeping a firm lid on overheads.

James McNaught-Davis, Managing Partner,
Sustainability Investors LLP, London

Jeremy Rudd delivers the goods in this very accessible and easy to read business book for everyone. Start-ups to Fortune 500 companies will appreciate the easy to remember approach and the ease at which it can be explained to their teams. His 4 Magic Steps are extremely compelling, Buy it, you can't afford not to!

Trevor Hill, former Chairman & CEO, Global Water.
Phoenix, Arizona.

Like a Master Chef, Jeremy has taken simple and fresh anecdotes, seasoned them with years of business experience, put them in the pot, and reduced them down to concentrated Steps, to nourish all businesses.

Andrew Milne, MD and owner Geotechnical
Engineering, Gloucestershire.

Businesses are
battling to survive

Taking a Magic Step will
make a huge difference

Contents

Introduction

The world is changing and becoming more and more challenging. In recent years we've encountered Covid-19, the acceleration of global warming and devastating floods and fires, all of which have impacted businesses large and small. But the business environment was volatile even before these global challenges. In fact, it's always been changing, and the businesses that succeed have always been the ones that reinvent their offering to adapt to the environment around them. Maybe you've been a little slow to do this in the past. As a result, maybe you've seen competitors who have used new technologies to reinvent their relationship with customers. Maybe they've taken advantage of your own customers, products and ideas and made them their own.

Amazon, eBay, Facebook, Google, Airbnb and Uber are often quoted as examples of the 'new economy', but thinking back, your rivals were probably beginning to offer cheaper, better, sexier products, delivered faster than you, long before the creation of these businesses. Now is the time to change, and fast.

But how?

Whether you are starting a business, relaunching or want to drive continual improvement, the first step is to always believe that you can do better. Stay vigilant, and continually assess how to improve or eliminate processes using new technology, AI and social media. For example, who would have imagined that the verb 'to Zoom' would be part of everyday language around the world? Continually look to improve your relationship with your customers, and remember that they are changing too.

This second edition of 4 Magic Steps to Double Profit still uses a story to demonstrate the fundamentals of improving profit and cashflow. By keeping the message simple and clear it picks through the complex and sometimes difficult decisions you need to make. But it's now updated to reflect the rapidly changing times we live in, and the ways customers are changing too.

Use 4 Magic Steps to develop and maintain a successful business that your customers and you will love. Let's create value together.

Jeremy Rudd
2020

Foreword by Prof Ruth Allen

Business agility, stability and profitability has never been more crucial…

In times of rapidly advancing technology as well as environmental, health and economic challenges, it's more important than ever for business owners and directors to run agile companies where creativity and innovation can flourish so that their businesses can be sustainable. It is also crucial that creativity and innovation does not flourish at the expense of the company's financial stability.

I have spent over 40 years delivering consultancy services to regulated and private infrastructure businesses worldwide. For many of those years I have had responsibility for profitability as a manager, director or chief executive. Through these years I have managed and grown businesses ranging from small start-ups to larger companies through good as well as difficult trading circumstances and learned the importance of "knowing and understanding my numbers".

Rising profit margins, a healthy cash flow and demonstrable growth in earnings have always been good indicators of a healthy business. You may perceive that your company is running along efficiently and that you are doing as well as you can – but how do you know?

As a business guru who has advised companies all over the world, Jeremy Rudd has an incisive instinct to be able to home in on the important or 'uncomfortable' issues in any business at great speed and with canny accuracy.

In Four Magic Steps to Double Profit, Jeremy demonstrates this focus and clarity. Through the telling of a charming and clear story he takes us 'back to basics' as we hear how an entrepreneurial young girl called Jo builds her first business with help from her Grandpa and Squawk. We learn from Jo's mistakes and successes.

As Jo starts to develop her business selling apples, she and the readers are introduced to a set of simple tools – the 4 Magic Steps – which focus on the important impact of price, sales, costs and fixed costs on profit and cash in a business. We learn with Jo as her business starts to become more complex. Jeremy brings common sense, practical examples and punchy learning points together and inspires you to take action in the way he has inspired businesses to grow and improve.

It has never been more important to nurture business agility, stability and profitability. Whether you are an experienced director or just about to take your first steps into the world of business, reading 4 Magic Steps will help you to ensure you are doing this. The focus on securing sales or minimising costs to make a profit to generate cash is the same in any business….and who wouldn't want to double their profits?

Professor Ruth Allen
Malmesbury - June 2020

Section 1

Focus: Why Every Business Needs a Target

E very business needs to stay focused. 4 Magic Steps gives you the tools to do so.

We often say, "If it isn't broke, don't fix it." But don't be fooled. It's quite likely that your business has deviated from its original target. But what is still relevant? Customer choices continually change, but old processes that were relevant to old customer demands tend to remain, meaning your costs could be higher than new entrants in the market.

Costs in business naturally escalate, but customers are focused. They want products at the best possible specification, for the best price, delivered 'now', and this can continually put pressure on your margin. That's why Magic Step 1 highlights the dynamic relationship between your products' selling price and your profit, while Magic Step 2 focuses on the effect of sales volume on your profit.

Gone are the days of being able to price inefficiencies into your selling price: customers will simply go elsewhere if you are not competitive. That's why Magic Step 3 shows why and how to continually trim costs to stay efficient.

Even the biggest companies can fail if they don't stay focused. Who would have thought Toys Яus would go bust or Hertz would go into administration? Magic Step 4 focuses on how fixed costs can lead to risk and failure, with guidance on how to refine your business model to maximise profit.

After each Magic Step Squawk will give you concise Action Points so you can quickly make a difference to your business.

But first the focus is on the business target. You'll see that when our young entrepreneur Jo leaves her job, her decision is whether to risk her regular salary for the 'joy' of running her new business. Running a business for fun isn't a clear target, and her first attempt fails because of it.

Is the original target for your business still valid? Section 1 emphasises the need to continually reassess, record and discuss success, failure and inefficiency, allowing you to adapt quickly to stay ahead of competitors.

Whether you are planning a new business, a side project or a business expansion programme, focus on your purpose for doing it. Is it to make money, or do you want to save the world, have a better lifestyle, get more flexibility or find better job satisfaction?

Whatever the reason, there has to be a target to focus on. And whether making money is the driver or not, making a certain amount of money has to be an outcome. Other objectives can be put on a side burner – having cash in the bank cannot.

You'll see that, by listening to Squawk's advice and following the Magic Steps, Jo more than doubles her profit. Understanding and using the 4 Magic Steps can help you to do that, too.

Finally there are Checklists at the back of the book to guide you through your business transformation.

Let's follow Jo on her journey.

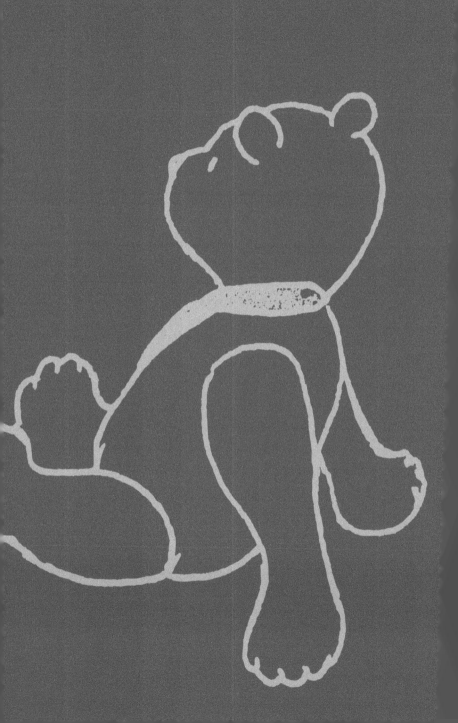

Section 2

SAVE ME: The Magic Business Formula

Let me introduce Jo, our aspiring young business entre-preneur. We meet her as she's assessing the opportunity of starting a new business whilst considering the risk of leaving her job.

Jo was getting through a busy afternoon at work. She hated being on the shopping mall, as she couldn't help but think about the carbon footprint of all the businesses around her. It was also hard work—she was just finishing another shift of working twice as hard for the same money because another member of staff had just left. It seemed her boss couldn't keep his staff.

Jo grabbed her bike and set off home, her teddy bear Mr Ted sitting on the handlebars to keep her company.

Jo was happy because the sun was shining and she had cash in her pocket, but she was sad because she wanted to run her own business. She just knew she could run a greener business selling fresh local produce that wasn't traveling across the world. She wanted to be better than her boss, selling local products without wasteful packaging whilst also making money AND being her own boss. But she was too scared to try.

Jo found herself cycling past her grandfather's house, so she thought she would stop and have a break as her legs ached from all the running around the shop. She sat by the house watching the little stream running down the road next to her. It was so nice with the sun warming her, the trees rustling. She lay down on the grass, closed her eyes and went into a deep sleep.

Startled, Jo suddenly sat up. Mr Ted was sitting next to her, leaning on her legs and eating a big apple. The juice was dripping off his chin. He looked at Jo and asked, "Do you want a bit? It's delicious"

Jo took a big bite and wondered where it had come from.

'It's free; I got it from Grandpa's orchard. There are lots, go and help yourself – but leave plenty for me!' Mr Ted laughed.

As Jo was eating her delicious apple Mr Ted said, "Here's the business you wanted! You could sell these apples and make a lot of cash. What do you think?"

Jo thought it was a great idea but told him that as it was his idea she would need to make him a partner to help her. Mr Ted quickly agreed, thinking about all the cash he would make.

"That's great, Mr Ted. I do need you because I would be scared to do it by myself. I don't know what to do…" Jo thought carefully. "But I'll do it – I'll set up my stall tomorrow. But first we need to talk to Grandpa."

Why do we need a target?

Jo was so excited that she rushed up the garden path, but suddenly she was overcome by nerves. Mr Ted had to push her.

Grandpa must have seen them because he was waiting at the door.

Jo said nervously, "Mr Ted and I have a wonderful idea for a business – I can stand at your gate and sell lots of apples from your orchard!"

Grandpa frowned. 'Why do you want to set up a business? What about your job?" he asked.

"I want my own business because I want to sell things that are local and fresh. I'm going to give up my job. Really, Grandpa, it doesn't pay well, the boss is awful and the things we sell are all mass-produced miles and miles away and transported to us, creating CO_2. Mr Ted says I only have to sell a box of apples a week to make more money."

Grandpa wanted to encourage Jo, but he also wanted her to learn, so he told her, 'First you need to have a product that is so brilliant your customers will go out their way to buy it. So be different, be special."

Then he added, 'Starting your own business is a RISK. Remember that currently you get paid for your job, day in, day out. You'll lose this regular cash and you'll still have things to pay for.

"Make a target, Jo. Be sure, for instance, that you can make more money than in your current job. After all, you'll be miserable if you don't have enough cash to pay your bills."

"All businesses must have clear targets," he shouted to her as she walked down the path. "Remember: no target, no success. Come back to me tomorrow to tell me how you get on."

Jo went to the orchard and got busy, picking all the apples and putting them away safely.

It was fun and exciting; she was finally her own boss, the start of something new, but she thought very hard about setting the target. It had to include making money.

Jo polished each apple lovingly. It was hard work and took many hours until she became exhausted, but by the end of the day her store was full of wooden boxes of apples. Mr Ted came along and laughed at all her hard work.

"You're wasting time – just throw them into a box," he laughed.

Jo was angry with Mr Ted "These apples are beautiful, they are straight from the orchard, fresh and with no carbon footprint. And besides, we must make our target. Our apples have to be the best to achieve that," she rebuked him.

The next day Jo set up a stall, but as she made her signs, she suddenly wondered what price to charge for the apples. She didn't worry too much and just decided to see how much her customers would give her, and anyway, Mr Ted had gone to sleep in the warm sunshine so she could not ask him.

As the sun went down Mr Ted woke up. He saw that the stall had been taken down and that Jo was about to go home. He smiled at Jo and said, "You must have done well! You have sold all your apples."

Jo was still on a high from having so many customers and selling all her apples, but she said "Yes, but I wanted your help, you promised you would. I needed another box of apples from the store as I had sold out. Anyway, here is your share of the cash as agreed; I'm off to see Grandpa."

Grandpa greeted her with a big smile. "How was your day?" he asked. Jo didn't know what to say, but nervously explained, "Well, I enjoyed myself. It was busy and exciting not having a boss, I was selling lovely local apples with no carbon footprint and my new customers were very nice, but I don't have as much cash as I normally do." Suddenly she was downcast. "What did I do wrong? SAVE ME, Grandpa."

Grandpa sat for a while before saying, "You've learnt a lot today. Sometimes entrepreneurs are too busy to work out how to do things properly before they set off, and that was your mistake too."

Grandpa stood up and asked, "Remember I talked about a TARGET? What was it?"

Jo remembered. "I promised to have more cash in my pocket at the end of the day than my normal wages."

"So, Jo," Grandpa said "Pick up the iPad and list what happened today."

Grandpa watched the screen on the wall as Jo wrote:

I sold lots of delicious local apples
Customer loved the apples
I was very busy
Not enough cash at the end of the day

Had fun
All apples sold
Customer took advantage of me
Could have sold more

At that moment a scary big bird flew in through the window, squawking loudly, and landed on Grandpa's sofa. Jo jumped up, frightened, but Grandpa said, "Don't worry about Squawk, I've worked with him for many years, as you can see he has fought his way to many victories in business," Jo saw the sticking plaster and wooden leg and realised how much experience he had. Grandpa continued "I asked him to come and help you."

Squawk squawked, "I was flying around watching you sell your apples. I could see customers grabbing lots of apples but not paying much. It is easy to sell things cheap, but that way you will always be a BUSY FOOL and will never make lots of money."

Frowning, he looked at the screen on the wall. Squawk got straight to the point, "Jo, remind me: why did you start your own business?"

Remembering her conversation with Grandpa, Jo knew what Squawk was aiming at: her target. "To sell beautiful apples and have more cash in my pocket than normal," she said confidently, but she was surprised when Squawk continued.

"And how were you planning to do that?' he queried.

"By selling lots of apples, of course," replied Jo indignantly.

Squawk laughed loudly. "But you did that today and you were left with less cash. Why?"

He continued "you didn't have a plan to achieve your target." He squawked rather loudly "How did you know how many apples to sell to reach your target if you hadn't worked out how much to charge for your apples?"

Jo suddenly realised it was because she didn't know how much to charge for the apples nor how many to sell. Quietly she said to Squawk 'I didn't work that out'.

Set a target and a plan

Grandpa quickly stepped in. "Jo, here are some rules to create a successful business":

1 Set and continually update a TARGET

"Neither entrepreneurs nor executives have focus unless they have targets (business plans and budgets). And you can only achieve your target with a plan."
He wrote on the screen:

NO TARGET, NO SUCCESS

2 Agree your PLAN

"Make a plan of how you are going to achieve your target by selling enough apples at a price you choose."
He added to the screen:

NO PLAN, NO TARGET

3 Find out what VALUE your customers place on your product. What PRICE will they pay?

"Knowing what price should you charge is vital because without a price you cannot make a plan to achieve your target."

"Your research must find out two things: first, before you start selling you should know the market. Who are your prospective customers? Does anyone want to buy your apples? Why do they want them? How much do they pay at the moment? How do they VALUE your apples – do they love them? In other words, how much are they prepared to pay?"

NO PRICE, NO PLAN

4 Establish the cost of your product

"The second is COST. Before you set a price, you must understand how much each apple costs – You will fail if you set a price less than cost.

Grandpa added the fourth and final point on the list:

NO RESEARCH, NO PRICE

Then he said, "So, Jo, sit down with Mr Ted and work out what to do next."

Jo quickly wrote down Grandpa's points to help her remember:

- Set a target
- Agree your plan
- Value your product
- Establish the cost

Jo was happy. She knew what she had to do but just as she was leaving Squawk said, "I need to make sure you don't forget the lesson of knowing how to price your apples and that they are not free, so I have asked Grandpa to charge you for them."

"He will charge you 10 cents for each apple, so that's the first cost you have to cover. Let's meet again tomorrow to make sure you have got it right. Finally, do not forget you need a profit to generate cash to invest in the business, like buying a new stall for instance."

"Do all of this, add up your numbers then discuss the results with your team. These are the final steps:

- Measure your success or failure

- Explain the outcome.

This will help us all learn from our experience."

"Thank you, Grandpa and Squawk, I asked you to save me and you have given me lots of advice, and I will use SAVE ME to help me remember what to do!"

Jo went off to tell Mr Ted what she had learned; she was exhausted but wanted to explain everything.

Mr Ted sat looking at Jo and laughed when he heard that Grandpa was charging her for the apples.

"Grandpa is going to get richer than you!" he giggled. But he listened to Jo as she explained what she had learnt.

"No, seriously, Mr Ted, today we learnt that pricing is important, without it we don't know how to make our target, unless we get it right our business will fail. I asked Grandpa to save me when I could not work out why there wasn't enough cash. SAVE ME is what we need to do!

- Set a target for what we want to achieve

- Agree a plan to achieve our target

- Value our product – do market research to see how much our customers value the apples so that we know the optimum price to charge.

- Establish the cost of our product, find out all the costs and using this and the market research price our apples

And then afterwards:

- Measure the success or failure and analyse outcome

- Explain the outcome with our team, Grandpa and Squawk; use any lessons to make tomorrow more successful

So Jo and Mr Ted talked about the business, and after assessing all the risks and opportunities they decided they could succeed by following the rules. They understood the first steps to achieve the target of running a successful business.

Squawk's action points

SAVE ME: Key building blocks for business success

- Use SAVE ME as a building block to success
  Put SAVE ME into your business's routine, get focused on achieving your target and measure and explain results to your team regularly.

- Before launching a business or project always have a focus
  Ask yourself: 'What is the target? What am I trying to achieve? Why am I doing this? What is the commitment required? Do I have the support I need?

- Continually check your business plan

Business never stands still, so continually assess that your plan is still valid. Question what has changed – the marketplace? The technology? The supply chain? The sales channel? The people around you? A "sniff test" is a simple and quick way to tell if your business is relevant, efficient and worth taking to the next level, and/or what modifications may be needed. It can save you a lot of wasted effort and resources and should take no longer than 30 minutes. Please see Checklist 1 at the back of the book for template.

Section 3
The Magic Steps

Magic Step 1

The Dynamic Relationship Between Price and Profit

Now that she had learnt how to price her product, Jo took charge.

"Mr. Ted, you need to research to see what VALUE people put on our apples. Go around all the shops in the area and find out how much they charge for their apples. Whilst you are there talk with the customers and ask them what would make them buy from us. You shouldn't be afraid of our customers," Jo added, "we have a wonderful product for them, the apples taste great, shine beautifully, are locally grown and not transported across the world. Off you go, I am polishing more apples for tomorrow."

"But first let's work out our costs. Let's aim to sell a box of apples a day. There are 100 apples in each box. We know Grandpa is charging us 10 cents per apple, so that's 1,000 cents, but what about the other things to cover?"

Mr Ted quickly said, "Well, we need to add the same amount of cash that you used to get from work – that's 500 cents, and of course there is my 500 cents as well."

Jo was thinking hard. "I wonder if we should put on something for profit?" she asked Mr Ted.

"I think Squawk would be furious if you didn't," replied Mr Ted.

Between them they agreed to add on 100 cents (5%) for profit, making a total of 2,100 cents. They look at the screen to make sure they understood the selling price.

Jo and Mr Ted agreed. Their selling price for each apple would be 21 cents.

For 100 apples	
Apples	1,000
Jo	500
Ted	500
Net Profit	100
Total	2,100
Selling price	21 cents

Market Research: Finding the Value

"Right, Mr Ted, you go off and find out how much the shops are charging, See if there is anything the customers may want which would add to the value they place on our apples, and if there is anything we could do to help them."

Market research is vital in all businesses

Mr Ted did his work diligently. Going to lots of shops – 'our competitors' Jo had reminded him – he looked at their range of apples, spoke to a lot of people and found there were many ways they could be different from the other shops. He went back to Jo and gave her the news.

"Jo, we could actually charge more than we thought, if we added value. Here are some of the customers' ideas.

We will have happy customers if we:

- Had the shiniest apples

- Emphasise low carbon footprint by sourcing the apples locally

- Visited each customer to see how many they wanted each week

- Delivered the apples to their house

- Gave away special recipe sheets, different ones each week for apple crumble, cake and other delicacies

- Sliced them up into easy to eat chunks

Set Your Price using Market Research

They agreed to try all of these ideas and they were also confident enough to raise their selling price to 22 cents. Jo revised her pricing calculations, and she quickly worked out that by putting their price up by just 5% **their profit doubled!**

For 100 apples	
Apples	1,000
Jo	500
Ted	500
Net Profit	200
Total	2,200
Selling price	22 cents

Jo was really pleased with Mr Ted's research and immediately revised her signs to 22 cents

Jo and Mr Ted now understood Magic Step 1: Even small changes to your price create a huge difference to profit.

Jo said to Mr Ted, "It's amazing that even small changes in the price we charge make a HUGE difference to profit. Profit dramatically changes when we move our price, just a 5% increase in price meant a doubling of profit!"

Squawk flew in and said, "You've just worked out the quickest and most powerful way of increasing profit! **You found out the dramatic relationship between the selling price and profit, that a 5% increase in price DOUBLES profit.**"

Squawk continued "Increasing your price is always dramatic, because your costs don't move. Depending on your margin you can increase profit dramatically." Squawk showed them a simple chart. He wanted everyone to understand how important price was in increasing profit.

Impact of increasing selling prices

	Existing NP Margin*			
	5 %	10 %	20 %	25 %
Increase your price by:				
2 %	40 %	20 %	10 %	8 %
5 %	100 %	50 %	25 %	20 %
10 %		100 %	50 %	40 %
15 %			75 %	60 %
20 %			100 %	80 %
25 %				100 %

*Your Net Profit

"Businesses that have a 5% margin like Jo's will see their profit DOUBLE with a 5% increase in price. Even a business with a 20% margin will increase profit by 25% if it puts up prices by 5%.

Beware of Discounts

Squawk wanted Jo to understand the dynamics of reducing her selling price as well.

He said 'You will at some stage be confronted with the thought of having a sales promotion in response to competitors' activity, but when planning to reduce prices for the sales promotion, make sure you don't forget Magic Step 1.'

'Jo, just as a small increase to your selling price has a huge impact on your profit, so does a small decrease, because your costs are still the same.'

Don't compete on price alone, that's lazy thinking!

'Jo, think carefully before reducing prices to get extra sales, because you will lose profit unless you can pass on reduced cost in your supply chain, thereby preserving your margin.'

Squawk continued 'If price is reduced in a sales promotion, you will have to work really hard to keep your profit. Depending on your gross margin, a small change to your prices will have a dramatic impact on your profit. If you have a 5% margin, a price reduction of just 2% means you have to sell 67% more to stand still.

Impact of reducing selling prices

	Existing business Net Profit			
	5%	10%	20%	25%
Reduce your price by:				
2%	67%	25%	11%	9%
5%		100%	33%	25%
10%			100%	67%
15%			300%	150%
20%				400%

To maintain profit you must increase sales by:

Even a business with a 25% margin would have to sell 67% more if they reduce price by 10%!" Jo understood the risk to her profit if she reduced her prices and told Squawk she would never do it.

"Come and see me if you are even thinking of doing it," he said.

Four Magic Steps to Double Profit

Squawk's action points

Magic Step 1:
Optimising price

- Markets change quickly, so be vigilant
  Always understand how your customers perceive value, as this changes all the time.

- Always get the last %
  Ask yourself: 'If we increased our prices by 1% would we lose that sale?' The answer is probably not. What about 5%? 10%? More?

- Focus your sales teams on margin
  Few sales teams are rewarded on margin – more likely their bonus is based on how much they sell rather than the profit they have created, and of course it is easier to close a deal at a lower price. But as we can see in the table above, even small increases in price have a huge impact on the bottom line. Check out the sales teams' incentives.

- Review prices regularly as your competitors change their offering frequently
  Don't put off reviewing prices regularly just because it's difficult. Continually check your selling price against competitors.

  Consider using a SaaS comparison price and quotation management provider to constantly compare your prices against others'.

- Don't be modest, be confident of your product and show your love for it

Never be afraid to charge the full price. If you have a premium product you don't need to beat the competitors' price. A higher price gives confidence.

Think: If you had a ground-breaking piece of technology and only charged 10% of the price of a rival, wouldn't your potential customers question the quality and capability of the product? It's all about whether the customer senses value.

Note: Your customers need to be reminded of the quality and superiority of your product.

> Always have an expensive offering to tempt your customers with, boosting sales and margin

- Find out what your customers value

Previously people just wanted their purchase to work and be cheap, like Ford's Model T car. But that's not the focus anymore. A product has to be fashionable, the best, the sleekest, the fastest, the greenest, preferably local, the easiest to use and available immediately. Price is now not always top of the list. So talk to customers today – what gets them buying your products?

- Don't be misled, how much your product costs to make is not important to the customer

In the buying process people assess price on what THEY will gain or lose, not how much it costs you to make.

Price is what the market can bear and the perceived value of the product. Customers make decisions about value – then they act.

- Always give options
  Offer a 'light' version for those with a tight budget, and at the other end offer extras to improve perceived value.

I sold ice cream in my school holidays, driving around the town and villages selling ice cream and cookies. Having small cones satisfied the customers with little cash but I also made sure there was plenty to add onto my basic 'Mr Whippy', such as chocolate sauce and ground almonds to get the price up for the premium ice cream, and of course the margin increased dramatically as the price went up. I used to give a free one to the first customer, because the customers behind them in the line saw them, were tempted, invariable buying it.

- Understand and value your customer
  Be aware of how sensitive your customers are to fashion and trends – don't assume their loyalty, reward them. Remember, it's likely that 20% of your customers will generate 80% of your profit. Do you really love your customers? Do you make them feel special?

- Let unprofitable customers go
  At the other end of the profitability list are customers who regularly moan about price, constantly call to complain, often return products and consume the energy of your business. Let them go – they are costing you money.

When I worked at a packaging factory in South Africa 95% of the net profit was made from only 20% of the customers. By culling the unprofitable ones the company ended up a highly profitable, nimble and customer focused leader of the industry. Work out a plan to cull nuisance customers today.

Warning

Don't measure performance on the value of sales alone. Products have different profit margins.

Think of your Gym.

Your annual subscription has a 100 % profit margin as the Gym is not incurring any extra costs with you as a member.

But if you paid the Gym the same for 1 2 1 coaching then only half is profit, the other half will go directly to the trainer

Both have the same sales value, but subscription goes all the way to the bottom line, but only 50 % of the coaching goes to the Gym's bottom line.

Four Magic Steps to Double Profit

Magic Step 2

The Dynamic Relationship Between Volume and Profit

The next day Jo persuaded Mr Ted to use her bike to go around the village visiting new and old customers. He would ask them how many apples they wanted and then he would deliver the apples on a Friday.

Jo worked on keeping the apples polished nicely. Sometimes, when she had time, she sliced up apples for Mr Ted to deliver to customers. She also got her Mum to write some recipes to hand out to her regular customers for them to use to make lovely apple cake and other delicacies.

Jo worked out who were her top 10 customers and sometimes she gave them some spices with the recipes to make them feel special.

Each time she went back to Grandpa with her report he was delighted with her progress.

One day he even surprised her when he analysed her cash surplus, because not only had they doubled profit by charging 22 cents, but on average they had sold 105 apples a day. With this 5% increased volume their profit had gone up again!

Jo was delighted and, thinking about how a 5% increase in price had DOUBLED her profit, she said, "So have we doubled our profit again Grandpa?"

Grandpa replies "I like your thinking, Jo, but this impact to your business is not as great as putting up price. When you put up your price, with each and every apple you sell ALL the extra cash is yours because your costs don't go up.

"It's different when you sell more volume, because you only keep the cash after paying your supplier (me) for the apple. So, in this case you are selling them at 22 cents and paying me 10 cents, so it means you get to keep 12 cents.

"Every day you are selling an extra 5 apples, meaning you will get 60 cents extra and your profit will go up from 200 cents to 260 cents – an increase of 30%, which is amazing as well."

Squawk, who had swooped in and was sitting on the window ledge, said "Jo, Grandpa has shown you Magic Step 2, make sure you always try to sell more."

Squawk's action points

Magic Step 2:
Increasing sales

- Add value to beat the changing competition
  Always look to see how you can add value to your products
  to get that extra dollar from your customer.

  Think of your mobile phone provider. What bundled
  add-ons do they offer you to increase the profit they make
  each month? What can you bundle into your offering?

- Make it easy for your customers to get what they
  want immediately
  Customers take a lot of time researching but once they
  have decided to buy your product, they want it now,
  Amazon has set the standard, allowing customers to buy
  today for delivery tomorrow. Check your sales distribution channel – is it the best? Can it be improved?

- Always spoil your loyal customers
  Never forget the people who have bought from you before.
  You already have their trust, and if they like you and/or
  your product they will be back. Talk to your customers
  to find out what else they may want from you.

  *A successful real estate company in Los Angeles always holds
  a champagne family Christmas party for all their clients to
  thank them for their business, a wonderful way to get like
  minded people together who undoubtably talk about how
  clever they are to buy a magnificent property investment.*

On the way out each client was handed almond and caramel-ized popcorn in a beautiful tin in their brand colours and logo.

Their clients will always think of them when talking to friends in the New Year about which company to use to help them find a new home / property investment.

- Keep focus. Customers are king, but fickle, and they'll move their dollar elsewhere if there is a product they value more

  Never rest on your laurels. Your product will not last forever as fashions and technology move onwards. Price will always be challenged. Innovate, experiment and keep asking customers what they want.

Four Magic Steps to Double Profit

Magic Step 3

Controlling Costs

Your business choice:
Finding the best leverage

CASH

Leveraging costs to get the best balance

Jo woke up having a panic attack. Yesterday she had introduced a new product: a chocolate apple flapjack biscuit she and Mr Ted had made themselves. But instead of making her usual 200 cents profit Jo had lost 920 cents! How? Where did all the cash go? Why did it happen? How will she sort it out before she loses everything?

Her mind went back to the beginning.

Mr Ted had been getting bored with just selling apples and he thought their customers were bored too: sales had fallen back to 2,200 cents a day on average. Of course, they were still making 200 cents on a daily basis, but he just felt they had to DO something. He had collared Jo to explain his thoughts.

So when Jo was having her daily meeting with Grandpa she had asked if he thought it a good idea to make something to sell alongside the apples.

He said, "Yes, remember Squawk's notes? It's a good idea to keep looking for ways to add value and have something new for your customers. But you must be focused. Don't lose sight of the successful business you have now – do it to increase your profit, not just because Mr Ted is bored. Reflect on your business plan.

Economic Activities

Grandpa was worried that Jo and Mr Ted did not have any experience of making things, so he said sternly, "Make sure you understand all the economic activities involved, count the cash carefully and report back to me."

Jo was confused. "What are economic activities, Grandpa?"

He replied, "Everything you do in business is an economic activity. For instance, picking apples, buying things and making things are all examples of economic activities."

Jo thought she knew what Grandpa meant and went to find Mr Ted.

Mr Ted was at home in Grandpa's old garden shed, keeping warm. "Come in, Jo, let's have a cup of tea".

Jo then explained she had talked to Grandpa about his idea of making some products to sell alongside the apples, she emphasised Squawk's comments about controlling costs.

Mr Ted said, "I've been thinking about this. Your Mum makes amazing flapjacks, why don't we sell flapjacks covered in lots of chocolate?

Jo liked the idea. It was another product that was fresh and made locally but she knew that chocolate was very expensive. She was worried. "We cannot just buy and sell chocolate, Mr Ted – everybody does that, we have to be different, we have to add value, remember our customers know us because of our apples."

"Eureka!" Mr Ted shouted. "let's make biscuits from chocolate, our apples, and mum's flapjacks! It will add value to our apples and everyone will love them."

> *"What's dangerous is not to evolve, not to invent, not to improve the customer experience."*
>
> **Jeff Bezos, founder of Amazon**

Ted's Idea Adds Value. Could yours?

It could take as little
as one minute
to think of a way to innovate to
add value to your product.

That's a brilliant use
of the next 60 seconds

"That's an amazing idea, Mr Ted," Jo continued, "What a wonderful fresh product, no additives and no allergens, perfect. We can make them in Mum's kitchen. I will write a recipe."

"But we will use chocolate CAREFULLY because it costs a lot of money and will take Mum a lot of time to make! Come with me, let's Google how to make them."

When they got to Mum's kitchen Jo said, "My Mum has special trays with lots of little individual moulds to make nice little chocolate biscuits. It looks like we simply put a little chocolate in, drop in the flapjacks, fill up as much of the remaining space with apple pieces and finally pour more yummy chocolate over them until we fill the moulds and scrape off any excess chocolate."

Mr Ted jumped up. "Does that mean I get to eat that wasted bit?"

Jo quickly said, "No, that goes back in to make the next one, otherwise you would get fat and we would lose all our money!"

"That reminds me Mr Ted, we have to decide what to do to make this a success: SAVE ME," she said.

Then together they filled in the answers.

Set a target	Add a complimentary product, using fresh ingredients and double the cash we make every day
Agree our plan of action	Jo to prepare a recipe to make biscuits listing the amount and cost of all the ingredients
Value the new biscuits	Mr Ted will visit shops to understand what value customers would place on our biscuits and compare what the competitors are doing
Establish the cost	Jo will calculate the cost of ingredients in the recipe. So that they understand how much a biscuit will cost
Measure and **E**xplain results	After the first day Jo and Mr Ted will add up the cash, understand the results, then explain to Grandpa and Squawk, and if necessary, make any changes

Jo went to the kitchen to create a recipe. She weighed and measured precisely a little of Mum's chocolate, some flapjacks and apple slices to put into each mould. She worked out how much it cost and what to charge, and quickly scribbled it down to make sure they followed the plan. "Squawk will be pleased," she thought happily.

Costing and Pricing the biscuits

For 100 biscuits

Chocolate	2,000
Flapjacks	400
Apples	40
Net Profit	260
Total	2,700
Selling price	27 cents

Jo's Mum gave her precisely the right amount of chocolate she needed for 100 biscuits. Mum asked who was going to make them and Jo realised that of course she could not be in two places at once, so she asked Mr Ted's friend Debra the dormouse to look after the stall whilst she and Mr Ted were busy. Whilst they were all there, they decided to call the biscuits Chockas.

Jo gave half the chocolate to Mr Ted. They each went to get the apple pieces and flapjacks that Jo had put out earlier and off they started, Jo at one end of the kitchen table and Mr Ted at the other. Jo made her Chocka biscuits carefully, putting in the first layer of chocolate then placing the flapjacks gently onto the chocolate. She added the pieces of apple onto the flapjack, making sure there was only space for a little of the expensive chocolate to finish it off.

Mr Ted, however, was in a rush because he didn't enjoy getting his fur messy and had to go to the shops to work out what price to charge, so when he poured in the chocolate sometimes he did not bother to put in a full flapjack or the apple pieces because it was so difficult and he kept getting his fur sticky.

"I'm finished!" shouted Mr Ted. "All my chocolate is gone!" He rushed off for a cup of tea then to the shops to check what prices everyone was charging.

Jo took her time to finish her Chockas. She was very proud of them and they all looked lovely. Whilst she tidied up she was a little surprised that there were some flapjacks and apple slices left over, and lots of crumbs with chocolate splashed around on Mr Ted's side. "I must tell him off," she thought angrily, "We can't make a mess in Mum's kitchen!"

Jo went to the stall to see how Debra was doing. "I hope you told the customers to come tomorrow for our lovely new delicacies," Jo asked.

Debra said she had done, but she added "I was so busy I needed to get a friend to help, because we had to deliver the apples that Mr Ted normally took to customers. I hope I did the right thing."

Jo replied, "Well done, Debra, thanks for doing that, I have been so busy I had forgotten."

When Debra heard how busy Jo was she suggested she took the cash to her house, which was below Mr Ted's garden shed. "My sister, Sage, lives there. She is brilliant at looking after cash and has lots of different tins to put the cash in."

Jo was delighted with the help because she was rushing around. She couldn't keep up, and Squawk had said she had to be vigilant with the cash.

Later, when Sage knew of her new responsibilities, she sent over two tins for the stall: one for apple cash and one for Chocka biscuits cash. She also knew she had to have a tin for all the different activities in the business.

Next morning, before the stall opened, Jo made some big signs. She had taken time to work out the price to charge based on the recipe. Mr Ted said, "The prices of biscuits in the shops nearby are much higher and you could charge more," but Jo didn't want to be greedy. She was happy with a 10% profit. "I want to be nice to our customers," she replied.

CHOCKAS
Yummy Chocolate,
Apple, Flapjack Biscuits
ONLY 27¢

Cashing Up

Jo was very excited. She and Debra worked busily all day, customers came and bought lots of the new biscuits, and even Squawk came along and bought some before everything on the stall sold. She was surprised how fast the Chockas had sold out – she was sure there should have been more. But there was lots of cash in the tins, so she was happy.

After tidying up, they went back to Mr Ted's, and gave the cash tins to Sage to sort out. Sage got busy with her tins: she had one for each cost and even had one for the profit.

Jo's Mum had told her the price of the flapjacks and chocolate, so Sage rushed off with two tins overflowing with cash to pay her. When she came back, she put cash into Jo's and Mr Ted's tins and also into Debra's. There was even a tin for Debra's friend who had helped her. She then got another tin for her own cash and all the rest went into Grandpa's. The pile of cash had become smaller all the time.

Finally, Sage said to Jo she must take Grandpa's cash to him. But when Jo had looked into Grandpa's tin, there wasn't enough cash! She shook the profit tin: it was empty!

"Sage, you must have made a mistake," Jo said, "Where is Grandpa's cash?"

Sage recounted the cash, checking all her tins, but everything was correct. She had put all the cash she had been given into the right tins; there was just not enough to fill Grandpa's.

She gave Jo a list of the tins and their contents so Jo could see what had happened to the cash.

Jo was shocked. She couldn't believe it, but asked Sage to take out cash from Jo's tin to make sure she had enough for Grandpa.

Sage's Tins

Sales Apples	2,200
Sales Chocks	2,430
Flapjacks	400
Apples	1,040
Chocolate	2,000
Debra	350
Debra's friend	150
Bean	150
Mr Ted	500
Jo	40
Profit	0

Jo looked at the list. She was so downcast she decided to go home and see Grandpa in the morning.

Jo came back to the present. It was not a nightmare – it had really happened. She had lost cash yesterday. She dragged her feet as she walked up to Grandpa's house; she was a little nervous because she knew there was going to be a discussion!

Grandpa looked wisely at Jo as he opened the door. "Jo, have you brought me my cash for the apples?" he asked. "You are late coming to see me, so I assume there is a problem, because there is a saying 'bad numbers take longer to add up!'"

"I have your cash, Grandpa, but we lost money. I don't know what happened. Where is it? How can I find it?"

Jo continued. "We have been very busy making things to sell; I even worked out how much to charge for them. We checked to see how much customers valued the new biscuits, everyone loved them, and we quickly sold all we made. But at the end of the day I had to take cash out of MY tin so that I could pay you!

I don't know where it's gone. Did I lose it at the stall or walking to Mr Ted's?" she wondered aloud. She felt tears coming into her eyes.

Jo was in despair trying to work out what happened

Grandpa said, "Don't panic, Jo, at least you know something is wrong – lots of businesses don't find out until it is too late – and you can pay all your bills, so it's not a disaster. What did you expect to have in your profit tin today?"

Thinking back to her plan, Jo got out the iPad and wrote:

I planned to have profit (surplus cash) from:

Sale of Apples	*200*
Sale of Chocka biscuits	*260*
Expected cash in the profit tin	*460*

Then she started to panic again as she remembered there was no cash in the profit tin. She even had to take 460 cents out of her tin to put into Grandpas, so that means in total they had a huge loss of 920 cents compared to the planned profit!

Huge loss

"How can we have lost so much just by adding a new product?" Jo was in despair.

HUGE LOSS
Expected cash   460
Jos cash to pay Grandpa 460
Total loss 920

Measure and Understand

Grandpa quickly interrupted. "Jo, calm down, let's get back to basics. It's all to do with BALANCE: what comes in must go somewhere, and what goes out must have come from somewhere! How much cash did you expect in total?"

Jo grabbed the iPad, writing:

Planned Sales

Apples	*2,200*
Chocka biscuits	*2,700*
Total sales	*4,900*

Grandpa said, "To get a balance, you need to compare how much cash ACTUALLY came in from your customers against how much you expected, so please go and get Sage's list of cash in the tins so we can work it out.

"This is really good," he encouraged her, "you clearly had a plan and that's where we have to start from. You were sensible to have Sage to help you—it means we will be able to find out, by looking in the tins what has happened. Well done so far!"

Balancing the Business

When Jo and Sage were back Grandpa said, "Take the iPad, write down all the costs for the apple business, and remember the sales were 2,200 cents."

Jo thought this was easy because she had seen it every day. She knew she had to pay Grandpa 1,000 cents and Mr Ted and herself 500 cents each. That came to a total of 2,000 cents.

Cash for Apples business

	Planned	Actual
Sales	2,200	2,200
Apples	1,000	1,000
Jo	500	500
Mr Ted	500	500
Net Profit	200	200

"Does it balance, Jo?" he asked.

Sage was jumping up and down, whispering to Jo. "It balances with the profit we expected of 200 cents!"

The Apples business made 200 cents profit as planned – it Balances

"That's it," Grandpa says with approval, "The Apples business balances!"

"So where did we lose the cash, Grandpa?" asked Jo. "We now know it wasn't from the apples business, so it must be from Chocka biscuits, mustn't it?"

Grandpa wanted this to be a learning experience for Jo and her team and replied, "Jo, go to your team, explain you have lost cash and see what ideas they have. But before you go, list all the cash you planned for the Chockas business."

Jo and Sage were quick to list all the planned sales and costs for the Chockas business.

Cash for Chockas business

	Planned	Actual
Sales	2,700	
Chocolate	2,000	
Flapjacks	400	
Apples	40	
Profit	260	

Squawk suddenly flew in through the window. "Grandpa," he said. "I think they need me to go with them to help, but first I'll let them make a start whilst you and I have a catch up."

Brainstorming : Where did the cash go?

Jo and Sage went back to Mr Ted's, where all the team were having a cup of tea. Jo explained that instead of having 460 cents in the profit tin there was none and she even had to take 460 cents out of her tin to pay Grandpa.

"This meant we have lost 920 cents compared to our plan," she said.

As they were still thinking Squawk flew in and sat on the table looking at them. "Carry on," he said, "pretend I am not here." They all laughed nervously.

Debra then said, "I went to the kitchen; it is shiny clean everywhere, no chocolate, no Chockas – so I went to Mum to see if she tidied them away and Mum said, 'I haven't seen any, but I do remember that when you came to collect the Chockas to take them to the stall there were 50 on Jo's tray but only 40 on Mr Ted's.'"

Squawk jumped down and said, "You only made 90 Chockas but you had enough expensive chocolate to make 100. Where did it go?"

Jo suddenly remembered Grandpa's words and told the team what he had instructed her. "Make sure you use your ingredients effectively. For the same amount you pay for chocolate you could get 50 apple slices or 5 flapjacks. Chocolate is the main ingredient as it has a lot more value. Use it carefully."

Jo worried about Mr Ted's biscuits. Why did he run out of chocolate making just 40 Chockas? Why were there apple slices and bits of flapjacks all over his end of the kitchen table? Jo said nervously to Squawk, "We don't know where the chocolate is. Did we use it?"

"You've just found Magic Step 3, Controlling and measuring your costs is critical," replied Squawk.

Measure the cost of ingredients

Squawk then told them, "Look at how you made your Chockas."

"How can we do that, Squawk?" asked Jo. "We can't go back in time."

"Aha, don't underestimate clever old Squawk. I bought some Chockas, don't you remember? I bought 2 from one tray and 2 from the other. If we cut them in half we can see how they were made. Who has a sharp knife? Let's see what they look like."

Squawk studies the biscuits

Squawk got Jo to carefully cut in half the biscuits from the first tray and said, "Look at these, they both look the same: lots of apple and a whole flapjack all covered nicely in chocolate".

Not making your product as specified loses cash and/ or customer satisfaction. Measure and analyse your numbers to find out what's really happening.

"Jo, this looks like the ones you made when you visualised yourself making Chockas. You did it precisely, measuring out each ingredient perfectly. But how about Mr Ted? What do you think?"

Jo, slightly trembling with nerves, cut the other Chockas in half. The team looked on with shock when they saw that the first Chocka was almost all chocolate. The second one was a little better, with half a flapjack and a little slice of apple.

It looked like Mr Ted had not put in enough apple slices or flapjacks and he had filled up all the empty space with expensive chocolate.

Jo now realised that's why Mr Ted ran out of chocolate after he had only made 40 Chockas and why some apple slices and flapjacks were left on the kitchen table when he had finished.

"What does that mean, Jo?" Squawk asked. Jo looked glum when she realised.

"Well, it means if Mr Ted did miss out the apple slices and flapjacks, which are cheap, the space was filled with expensive chocolate,

"You only sold 90 Chocka biscuits but used all the chocolate and wasted apples and flapjacks which had to be thrown into the green bin." Squawk moaned.

"This is why Magic Step 3 is so important. If you don't make your products to the planned specification you will be out of balance, losing cash and/or customer satisfaction."

Squawk asked what the planned outcome was for Chockas. So Jo showed Squawk what she had written for Grandpa on the iPad:

Chockas plan for the day:

	Planned
Sales	2,700
Chocolate	2,000
Flapjacks	400
Apples	40
Profit	260

Squawk told them "Put what actually happened, because you sold fewer but still used all the ingredients"

Cash for Chockas business

	Planned	Actual
Sales	2,700	2,430
Chocolate	2,000	2,000
Flapjacks	400	400
Apples	40	40
Profit	260	(10)

Out of Balance

Squawk summarised: "Instead of making a profit of 260 cents, you had a shortfall of 10 cents, making a total loss against plan of 270 cents."

Squawk emphasised 'The loss of 270 cents is caused by two reasons. First, let's understand what the outcome would have been if you had made and sold 90 Chockas perfectly in line with the specified ingredients."

90 Chockas

Sales	2,430
Chocolate	1,800
Flapjacks	360
Apples	36
Net Profit	234

Planned profit from making 90 perfect Chockas

Squawk went on, "If you had made and sold 90 perfect Chocka biscuits to your specification you would have used 2,196 cents of ingredients, but yesterday you used all the ingredients, costing 2,440 cents to make 90. This means you wasted ingredients worth 244 cents."

90 Chockas

Sales	2,430
Chocolate	2,000
Flapjacks	400
Apples	40
Net Profit	(10)

Actual loss from making 90 Chockas was 10 cents

Squawk wrote another fact:

Jo spent 11% (244 cents) too much on ingredients

"But you also lost the profit on the 10 Chockas that you didn't have to sell."

10 Chockas

Sales	270
Chocolate	200
Flapjacks	40
Apples	4
Net Profit	26

Lost Sales

Squawk pointed at the iPad 'That's another 26 cents you lost, making a total loss of 270 cents."

Squawk wrote another fact:

Jo lost 26 cents on 10 Chockas she didn't have to sell

"Excess ingredients came to 244 cents; the missing sales lost you 26 cents of planned profit, so you lost 270 cents."

Jo lost 270 cents

Chockas results

Excess ingredients	244
Lost sales	26
Lost Cash	270

Squawk continued. "By using just 11% more ingredients than in the recipe your profits were down by 244 cents. Sales were reduced by 10% compared to plan, and therefore your profits fell by 26 cents'."

Squawk flew off and Jo went home to try to understand it all, but she was still worried. She now knew why she had lost cash, but something else was missing.

Squawk's action points

Magic Step 3:
Control and destroy unnecessary costs

- Processes are changing all the time

  Businesses continually evolve, deviating from original plans. Check your business to ensure you are in line with your plans.

- Keep the business in balance

  Cash slips away very quickly, so keep vigilant at all times. Ask what is happening to your cash. Remember: **cash doesn't lie.**

- Always give your customers exactly what you advertise

  Measure ingredients/activities precisely against your product/service specification for the day's production. Do this by volume and cost to keep check on any deviations from your plan. I was in a paint factory that was losing money, using more ingredients than specified for the output. A while ago they had dodgy weighing machines and were told by their managers to fill the tins with an extra 5% to ensure they were not giving less than advertised on the tin. Even after the weighing machines were fixed operatives still gave the extra 5% because 'that's what we always did'. So customers were getting 5% more than they realised for free and didn't even realise or appreciate it.

- Suppliers are key to your input price

  Remember that costs fluctuate all the time, and not keeping track can cause your business to lose money quickly. Watch out for currency movement.

- Have a detailed business plan for each aspect of your business.

  Make sure you regularly monitor your performance against your plan, and don't be afraid to reassess your target. Invest in a 'Sage' to keep the business focused.

- Always be vigilant on your costs

  When did you last review all your activities and challenge them? You probably don't need 20% of them.

- Keep the business simple (1)

  Look at all your economic activities and see how they can be made more efficient or removed. Airlines are a great example: passengers now do all the ticketing, allocation of seat numbers, check in and luggage labelling. This reduces their costs which they can pass on to the traveller by providing cheaper flights.

- Keep the business simple (2)

  Let your customer use your App to order products or update their account, this keeps your costs down whilst providing a great gateway to them.

- When developing and launching a new product, always review your pricing assumptions

Don't assume your original plans remain in place. Instead, constantly review the balance. If necessary, review your processes to reduce costs so that you can have a lower price and/or increase your price to cover extra costs assuming market research shows that you will get sales at the higher price.

- **Don't be frightened to change if things are not working**
  Invest in restructuring your business. The returns will probably be much higher than acquiring a new business.

- **Do regular economic activity reviews.**
  Ensure all your economic activities are appreciated by your customer. Otherwise, why do it? A nationwide technology company had a department of service engineers who were working within their cost budget and getting praised for it BUT the business had not realised their customers didn't value this service anymore. Within the overall bundled price there wasn't enough cash to cover this element, it was therefore uneconomic. For a small discount the customers were happy to forgo this service: it was closed resulting in huge savings for the business. A win win – both parties reduced costs.

Magic Step 4

Fixed costs are a risk and time is your enemy

Jo's head hurt. She knew something else was missing. "We lost 920 cents, but only know what happened to 270 cents. Where's the rest?" she said to herself, confused. So off she went to Grandpa. She knew he would gently put her on the right track.

When Jo asked Grandpa, he agreed. There was still something missing that had eaten her cash, because the profit from selling her normal apples had disappeared as well. Grandpa wrote on the screen:

Expected cash – disappeared	460
Cash shortfall – Jo had to subsidize	460
Total lost cash compared to plan	920

Where did it go?

Wasted ingredients	244
Missing cash on lost Sales	20
Unknown loss	650
Total lost cash	920

Grandpa asked, "Where did the rest of the cash go? Think of all the activities that were going on and see where your cash may have gone.

Jo had been so busy she hadn't thought of all the help she had called upon – and she hadn't thought about where she was going to get the cash to pay them.

The only way to do that was to charge a proper price for the Chocka biscuits, and of course to make the Chocka biscuits to the right specification in the first place.

Grandpa said, "Look at Sage's list." When Jo took out Sage's list she realised her cash had to go a lot further. There were other people to pay:

Debra	350 cents
Debra's friend	150 cents
Sage	150 cents

All of these costs arose because Jo and Mr Ted were so busy making the Chocka biscuits. Jo turned to Grandpa and said glumly, "I was so busy I forgot to update the price of Chockas to cover the extra costs I had added to the business."

"Exactly." said Grandpa. "You didn't list those extra costs when you worked out a price for the Chockas.

Jo realises she forgot to update the Chockas' price to cover all the extra costs

"Business is always changing, so make sure your prices are up to date, keeping track of any new costs. Your price should have included all the costs involved, so what should you have set as the selling price?"

Jo got out the iPad and listed all the costs for Chockas:

Selling Price for actual production	
Chocolate	2,000
Flapjacks	400
Apples	40
Debra	350
Debra's friend	150
Sage	150
Total cost	3,090
Profit	309
100	3,399
Price for 1	34

Calculating the selling price for 100 Chockas

Jo said gloomily, "I should have been charging 34p but only charged 27 cents, and I could have because Mr Ted's market research said we could. No wonder I lost cash."

"Let's list what we have learned," Grandpa suggested to Jo.

Jo firstly wrote:

- I lost 7 cents on each Chocka we sold because I did not include all the costs when setting a selling price

Then she wrote down all the learning experiences:

- We wasted cash because we used expensive chocolate instead of cheaper apple slices and flapjacks

- The leftover apple slices and flapjacks were wasted because they would not be fresh for the next batch

- Last minute costs were forgotten, I did not include them in our pricing calculations

- We should have charged 34 cents but only charged 27 cents, even though Mr Ted said our price was much lower than the other shops

"But," said Grandpa, "think of the positives:"

- You now know that Chocka biscuits sell well, as they sold out in an hour

- Because of Mr Ted's research you know your customers will pay more for the Chockas

- You now know how to make them properly

- You now know that you must manage your staff to make Chockas in line with your recipe

'However,' Grandpa continued 'The lessons learned today can be summarised in our Magic Steps: Even small changes in the price you charge for your product can make a HUGE difference to your profit. So always know and include your costs when setting your price."

"Also. changes in the volume of your sales quickly affect your profit. So be vigilant: not hitting your planned sales will reduce your profit.

"Finally, control your costs. Not doing so will wipe out profit, so make sure you make your products to your recipe/specification."

Fixed costs are very sticky

"But that's only Three Magic Steps," Jo said.

Grandpa replied "Yes, you have learnt about costs in production but what about overheads – your fixed costs? These are the ones that are there whether you sell any products or not. You must always be vigilant of costs all around your business, and fixed costs are going to be with you for a long time, so be careful about bringing them into the business."

> *Fewer fixed costs =*
> *lower breakeven =*
>
> **The earlier in the day**
> **you make a Profit**

Squawk flew in. "Jo, how are you going to improve the business? Look at all the economic activities and see if they are necessary, whether they are efficient and how they can be simplified or eradicated. You must get the balance right, Jo. Focus on each part of the business.

"Do you run the business in the most efficient way, at the lowest risk? Are your customers satisfied? Are they getting the best deal?

Time: the enemy of business

Squawk continued, "Remember: time is the enemy because fixed costs need to be paid regardless of whether you are selling anything, so every minute of the day you must be asking how you are going to cover the costs. The apple business is making 200 cents from sales of 2,200 cents, but the fixed costs are 1,000 cents so you don't cover your costs until nearly 3pm in the afternoon."

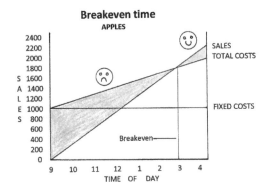

Not happy until 3pm

"Your fixed costs are high, which means waiting until halfway through the afternoon before you start making a profit. Think of the risks of that.

"What about the risk of selling less than planned? What if you sell 10 fewer apples? The answer is you will have to wait until nearly closing time before you cover your costs, meaning you won't make much profit that day. This shows how risky it is to have high fixed costs, because time runs out, but fixed costs stay forever.

Selling 10 fewer apples means you have to wait until after 4pm before you make a profit

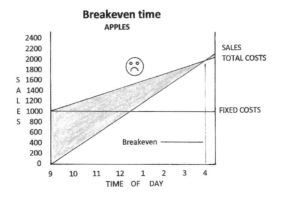

Breakeven time

Worried until closing time!

Squawk continues "In business you must review all your costs, so you should do that now. Is your team too big, too expensive?

> *"If you can't feed a team with two pizzas, it's too large."*
>
> ***Jeff Bezos, founder of Amazon***

For instance, you paid Debra's friend 150 cents for doing Mr Ted's job, but you pay him 500 cents. Also, is it fair that all your costs go against selling apples? What about Chockas? Finally, Jo, you are very expensive. What are you going to do about it? Could you make the Chockas more cheaply than you did today?"

Then Squawk highlighted an obvious fixed cost: "I don't think making things is Mr Ted's skill set, and YOU didn't train him to make the Chockas properly. He didn't realise that not making things as instructed would lose cash. Maybe get someone else to make the Chockas. That could reduce your risk and be cheaper as well."

"But I don't want to fire Mr Ted;" Jo said, "he's my inspiration; he is the creative one."

Squawk replied, "You must do the best for the business and your customers. Mr Ted is a fixed cost and expensive. Think about letting him remain the creative partner, allowing him to stay in bed and dream, but reduce his pay to, say 150 cents. I am not saying get rid of him – just use him to the best of his ability whilst making sure your business is run efficiently. Doing nothing will result in neither of you making money.

"He is still involved as he gets 50% of all the profit," Squawk reminded Jo. "That means that you now have 350 cents left to contribute to Debra and her friend's costs."

Squawk continued with his questioning. "I notice that customers are being pinched by your competitors and are a little more hesitant about buying apples from you, so apple sales are under pressure. How can we encourage customers to still buy apples or indeed increase the sales

> *"Education is the most powerful weapon which you can use to change the world."*
>
> **Nelson Mandela**

to them and others? A simple way is to reduce the price BUT only reduce the price if you can reduce the cost. We cannot afford to reduce our margin.'

'Have you thought of buying the apples elsewhere? I know our neighbour has plenty to sell."

Jo was getting exhausted as Squawk continued. "Look at all the costs – Debra did your job with ease and only charged 350 cents. As she sold Chockas as well, you should share her cost between apples and Chockas, 175 cents each. Her friend charged 150 cents for doing Mr Ted's job, so build that into the price – but don't forget that your salary and Mr Ted's are FIXED COSTS and must be priced in as well. Don't forget any costs this time!"

"So, I suppose I need to add in Sage's costs too?" Jo said.

"Well done Jo, yes you do. Now that covers all the activities, and remember these fixed costs need to be covered by the profit from your products each day. If you don't sell all your Chockas one day you can sell them the next day, **but your fixed costs are sticky – they have to be paid each and every day regardless of how many products you sell.** Make sure you cover these costs early in the day."

> *"The only thing worse than training your employees and having them leave is not training them and having them stay."*
>
> **Henry Ford**

Squawk told Jo to quickly reorganise the business before the morning, otherwise more cash would disappear. Then he flew off.

After paying Debra Jo found Mr Ted in his little home lying on his bed. He looked very unhappy.

"Hey, Mr Ted, Grandpa said you had an amazing idea creating Chocka biscuits. He thinks you are clever." Mr Ted's eyes suddenly started to shine again.

"You mean I'm not in trouble?"

Jo said, "No, of course not Mr Ted, you were the inspiration for us to do all of this, so you're not in trouble. But next time we must be disciplined in how we make the Chocka biscuits, because last time we put too much chocolate in."

Mr Ted understood what had gone wrong. "I didn't realise the value of the ingredients I was using. I didn't understand the huge price difference between each of the ingredients that went into Chocka biscuits. Now I know."

Jo admitted she got it wrong as well because she didn't include any labour costs when working out the price to charge.

"To be fair, Mr Ted," Jo added, "I admit I hadn't trained you how to make the Chockas or told you the consequences of using expensive chocolate instead of cheaper flapjacks or apple slices."

> *"Train people well enough so they can leave, treat them well enough, so they don't want to."*
>
> **Richard Branson**

Consider outsourcing to reduce costs and risk

Mr Ted suddenly said, "But you know what, Jo? I am not good at that sort of thing. Why don't you get some of Debra's friends to bake the Chocka biscuits with you and I will go away and create new ideas for us?" Jo was relieved that Mr Ted suggested his move first! 'That's fine Mr Ted, I will however have to reduce your pay to be able to afford someone else to make them, but don't forget that you get 50% of all the profit." Mr Ted replied, "Yes, that's fair and I am happy to do my new role"

Next, Jo followed up on Squawk's instruction to review all costs. She went to discuss making Chockas with some of Debra's friends to see if they wanted to become the Chocka mouse team, making the Chocka biscuits to her exact specification. They soon came back to Jo offering to make Chockas for 25 cents each, based on the costs from Mum for the chocolate, flapjacks and apple slices, but they wanted a minimum order of 200 per day because they had negotiated a rebate from the chocolate supplier if Mum bought twice as much. Mum agreed to do the same with the flapjacks, and the team of mice said they would make the Chockas in their own house with their own equipment.

Jo was delighted but decided to negotiate a little. "I'll agree this price if you deliver them to the stall every morning." Everybody was happy, so they shook hands in agreement. Jo had reduced the costs and risk, as fixed costs had been converted into direct costs and saved a lot of cash, risk and worry.

Outsourced Activities

6 Economic Activities gone:
- Buying chocolate
- Buying and preparing Flapjacks and apples
- Negotiating with Mum
- Making the Chockas
- Cleaning the kitchen and implements
- Delivering the Chockas to the stall

Jo wanted to see if she could reduce the price of the apples as well, so she took Squawk's advice and went to see Grandpa's neighbour, where she negotiated a 30% reduced price compared to Grandpa. The neighbour was delighted to sell his apples and was prepared to charge 7 cents an apple. He would even wash and shine the apples before delivering them to the stall each morning. Importantly Jo was able to negotiate deliveries all year round because the neighbour agreed to pick and store enough apples.

Outsourced Activities
5 more Economic Activities gone!
- Picking apples
- Storing apples
- Washing them
- Polishing them
- Delivering the apples to the stall

Jo asked Squawk if she was doing the right things. He was delighted and said it was the right thing to do. "But what about Grandpa?" Jo said, "Won't he be angry I am not going to buy the apples from him?"

"Don't worry, Jo, he will be impressed that you are looking at ways to improve your business by reducing costs and economic activities. And anyway, he wouldn't want to do all of those extra activities and he doesn't have enough apples to supply you all year."

- Never be afraid to haggle
  Suppliers build in additional margin to allow for this.

- Play suppliers off against each other
  Always be prepared to walk away from a deal.

- Never be scared to make a counteroffer which is way too low
  You have to find out when they will say no. Cash is precious; spend company money as if it were your own.

Squawk continued, "Let's review the new business model."

Jo was excited to show Squawk what she had prepared with Sage. "Sage and I went through our SAVE ME routine, as we didn't want to make the same mistake as last time. I went out and negotiated new deals that would reduce the cost of our ingredients and also ensure we get good quality products."

Jo was quick to report how well she had done. "We separated the costs into DIRECT COSTS, which vary with the quantity sold, and FIXED COSTS, which would be the same all the time regardless of whether we sold half the apples and Chockas or all of them. These are the sticky costs which include Mr Ted, Sage and me. I now realise these costs never go away: they have to be paid each and every day."

"Well done, Jo," said Squawk, "You've found out Magic Step 4: Minimise fixed costs because they are very sticky and have to be paid every day regardless of how many items you sell.

Squawk said, "Treat fixed costs like malware on your computer, virus check them ruthlessly and frequently."

Jo smiled. "Importantly, we decided to add a 20% margin to the price because we realise now that we are taking more risks and need to build up a reserve. So we put up the price of the Chockas, but not by as much as you would think – and they are still cheaper than the local shops!"

Squawk was very impressed, but he couldn't resist saying, "Jo, you are very expensive, especially as you have all these new helpers doing all the work. Your apple supplier is even polishing, shining and delivering your apples to the stall, which means you have very little to do! Maybe you should cut your salary to the same as Debra's?"

Jo agreed. She understood the logic and she also thought the message would help the team to understand how important it was to keep all the costs controlled.

Sage quickly changed the numbers and put them on the screen so Squawk could comment.

Pricing for Chockas

Chockas		5,000
Other costs:		
Debra 50%		175
Fixed costs		
Joe 50%		175
Ted 50%		75
Sage 50%		75
Total cost		5,500
Profit	20%	1,100
Estimated Sales	200	6,600
Price for 1		33

Make profit earlier in the day

Squawk asked to see the timeline again, so Sage drew a new graph for the Chockas.

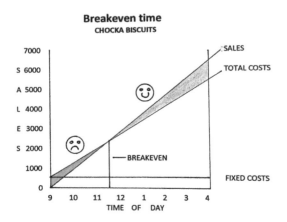

Breakeven time
CHOCKA BISCUITS

Cover your costs before lunch!

Squawk looked at the Chocka numbers carefully. "The pricing looks right, you have reduced risk by controlling the fixed costs, and you only have to sell about 30% of the Chockas to cover your costs, so by 11.30 you are making a profit. Well done!"

Then Sage put the apples business numbers on the screen.

Pricing for Apples

Apples		700
Other costs:		
Debra's friend		150
Debra 50%		175
Fixed costs		
Joe 50%		175
Ted 50%		75
Sage 50%		75
Total cost		1,350
Profit	20%	270
Estimated Sales	100	1,620
Price for 1		16

Let's see when we cover our costs for the apples:

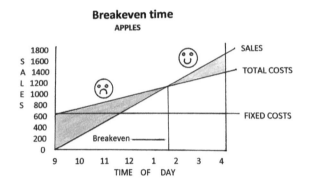

Breakeven time
APPLES

Breakeven before 2pm

Squawk again looked on intently. "Mmm," he said, "Looks a little risky. I think you may have reduced your price too much because your fixed costs are high in comparison to sales. You have to sell over 70% of the apples before you cover your fixed costs. If you can, decrease your fixed costs or increase the price to 19 cents. Remember Magic Step 1? Even small changes in the price you charge for your product/services can make a HUGE difference to your profit. Increasing the price to 19 cents will double your profit and you will cover your costs earlier in the day.

Jo agreed, after all, this still meant she had reduced the price by 15% compared to the 22 cents she charged before and she quickly got Sage to change the calculations.

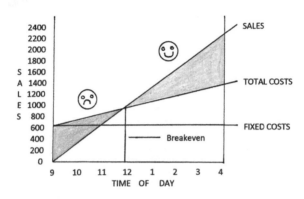

Breakeven time
APPLES

SALES
TOTAL COSTS
FIXED COSTS
Breakeven

TIME OF DAY

Happy before lunchtime!

As time moved on there were lots of dormice for Jo to train in baking and Mr Ted went and sat in the sun and thought a lot.

Jo had put the price of Chocka biscuits up to 34 cents (she added a little more because she was worried about wastage, some Chockas going missing or being broken), which was still competitive according to Mr Ted's research.

When customers asked why the price had gone up, Jo replied, "Yesterday was an introductory offer. You were lucky, and as a special bargain I have put apple prices down! Enjoy your day."

Squawk's
action points

Magic Step 4: Control fixed costs

- Businesses rapidly change but fixed costs are with you forever
  Be cautious, and take on new overheads as a last resort

- Continually review all your fixed costs
  Confirm they are adding value to your customer offering. Be vigilant: businesses always change and no product remains dominant forever. Don't get caught with overheads that are not appropriate for new products. A brewery in Cameroon I worked for was losing money. There was a crisis in the country and people couldn't afford the beer. Sales were down 30%, so we looked at all activities within the business to identify how we could reduce or eliminate costs to get a profit again. For instance, fixed costs had stayed the same even when sales had reduced so dramatically. Firstly, we undertook an Economic Activity Review. One activity we focused on was completed by a team of employees whose job was to dispose of used ingredients (grain, a valuable cow fodder). We assembled the team and offered to set them up in business to take, sell and deliver the grain to local farmers. It was a win-win situation: they got a business with the sales and we guaranteed no cost for the grain. We got rid of an expensive fixed cost reducing business risk, there was no cost if sales went up or down. A win win.

- Do not take on any fixed costs

  They have to be paid every day regardless of how many items you sell. Only take on fixed costs if you have researched all options for a direct cost option. For example, consider buying computing power from the cloud rather than investing in servers. Always have a review point in your capital expenditure requests.

- Outsource activities

  Continually review all business activities and outsource where possible, converting fixed costs into direct ones. However, make sure you rigorously monitor their performance on a regular basis.

- Challenge all supply agreements

  Can the cost of your ingredients or products be bettered? When did you last sit down with your key suppliers to see if there was a way to reduce their price? Consider buying in bigger batches to reduce unit cost, but not excessively so you carry too much stock.

- Ensure continuity of supplies

  Make sure you have product to sell all year round because overheads are there 365 days of the year.

- Always have a proactive Sage

  Real-time reporting means you can learn from your activities and rectify mistakes straight away.

Summary

Grandpa invited Jo to have a cup of tea with him to discuss the journey they had travelled.

Jo was happy she was now making a profit of 1,640 cents a day compared to the 100 cents in her very first plan. Even more importantly, all of her learning was focused around the 4 Magic Steps.

Squawk flew in and squawked, "Be careful Jo, you mustn't be complacent because business always changes. Be vigilant: there are always competitors out there who will try everything to pinch your customers, Check every day that you are efficient, what your competitors are doing and how happy your customers are.

Checklists

Checklist 1: The Sniff Test

Whether you're starting a new business or running a mature one, challenge the basics regularly. Take 30 minutes to ask obvious and basic questions, flush out scope creep, unnecessary activities and team pushback. If it smells bad, it probably is! Remember: if your competitors have lower costs they will always be able to undercut your prices.

Action
Write down your target/mission goal/time scale
For it to be relevant: We want the best organic chocolate biscuit on the market, to be the number 1 biscuit sold locally within one year and then to have it sold via all the supermarkets in the country within three years

Comments

Action
Describe the product/ service
For it to be relevant there must be a compelling story behind it

Comments

What is different/unique about your product/service.

There are always great ideas: innovative, sexy things that seem like they would just have to make money. That is your 'baby' and others may not love it as much as you do. What matters is whether many people will want to buy it at the right price. What is their assessment of value?

Comments

Who are your customers?

Describe a typical customer and how you could reach them.
Why will they buy your product?
How many will they buy?
How do you find out?

Comments

Is it easy to make/create? Is it made in house, or third party/offshored? What risks are involved in the supply chain?

How long will it be before you reach volume production? Remember: time is money.

Comments

Who are your competitors? What will they do to react?

Once you become a threat, they will do something!

Comments

Do you hold any patents, are any others filed?

Should you register a patent?

Comments

Action

What are the risks (what keeps you awake at night)?

Comments

Action

What is the best, most optimistic outcome?

Comments

Action

How much cash will you require to invest before the business becomes cash positive? What is the payback period? i.e. when will you pay off the investment from it's profit?

Comments

Is the team in place? Are processes and procedures in place, and are they in line with specification? If not in place how will you create the team. How risky is it?

Comments

Finally: Are you (and your team) 100 % motivated and committed to the business idea?

Comments

Now discuss this with someone you trust who is dispassionate and can discuss the outcome objectively with you.

Checklist 2: Review your Prices

Often price lists are left unchanged for months without review. Depending on your business it may be necessary to review your prices on a daily or weekly basis. Remember: your customers are always checking prices! Of course, there are many dynamics to be considered, so review all your products by asking these key questions:

Action

What date did you first release the product?
When did you last do an in-depth review?

Comments

Action

Has there been any investment in the product? When?
How much was invested (don't forget to price internal
resources), what was return on investment?

Comments

Action

Is investment required? How much? Over what period?
What is the estimated return on the investment?

Comments

Action

Are any new versions/releases due soon?

Comments

Action

Where does it stand in your top sellers list?

Comments

Action

What % does it represent of overall sales?

Comments

Action

What is the current selling price?

Comments

Where is its price point compared to competitors?

Comments

How many have you sold since your last review?

Comments

What is your current margin?

Comments

What is your total margin generated from the product since it was launched?

Comments

What has been the impact of any special offers/dis-counts offered?

What does your customer feedback say? Check for returns and/or credit notes raised and find out why.

Has there been any change to your input price (cost) since the last review?

Can the input cost be reduced?
When did you last challenge it?

Action

How long is your supply chain, and is it efficient?
How can you improve it? Can you invest to improve it?

Comments

Action

Update your market research, competitors' activity,
and assess any new products on the horizon.

Comments

Action

What is the value of stock held? At current sales levels
how many days' stock is held?

Comments

Once you have this information brainstorm the
opportunities to reset a new selling price. How will you
do it? Choose several and debate the pros and cons.

Checklist 3: Increase Sales

Be active in promoting your products. Customers are consistently searching and comparing, so be proactive by following the steps below:

Action

Review your customers and assess how to increase their spend, Remember: once they are customers, they have already formed a relationship with you. What do you need to do to help them buy more?

Comments

Action

Review your customers' customers. You may be selling to the end user through a sales distribution channel, so check to make sure the channel is working. Is there a better (cheaper, quicker) option of reaching the final consumer? Can you go direct?

Comments

Action

Consistently update your market research. Have you reached saturation point? Are there any gaps in the market? Are there other markets? Don't be complacent – always check. How will you do it?

Comments

Action

Find other customers, maybe in a different geographical area. How will you reach the customer? What other channels are available to you? What is the cost and payback?

Comments

Action

Would a price reduction increase demand? First check how you can reduce costs and pass those savings on to your customer. Don't be lazy – work on it. What costs can you squeeze out?

Comments

Action

Review your distribution channel. Remember what your customers want and make it easier, faster and cheaper for them to get hold of your product. What approach will you adopt?

Comments

Action

Review your marketing. Are your techniques efficient? Maximise social media options. They are always changing, so stay vigilant. What is the cost per new customer sale as a result?

Comments

Checklist 4: Test your reasons for reducing selling prices

Reducing your prices is the easiest and laziest way to respond to market forces, so before you allow any reductions to your selling price answer the following:

1   Has there has been any reduction to your input cost? If so you can pass the savings on to your customer without hurting the margin

2   If not sold, would the product be wastage due to sell-by dates? Check your stocking policy if this is frequently happening

3   Are there any product updates on the horizon? If a new release is imminent it could lead to obsolete stock in the future. However, remember that new product releases are notoriously late in arriving. Don't risk months or even years of discounting your 'old' product range before the new range is available.

4   Why is the business reducing prices? Is it because it's desperate to release cash from its stockholdings? If so this is a negative, defensive reason and needs to be understood. Quickly set in motion a business review (a sniff test) to assess business viability around your pricing/product/market policy

Checklist 5: Check activities and costs are necessary

Sometimes businesses think they're too busy to drill into the detail on a regular basis. This is foolish because life changes, sometimes daily. Continually test your business model and see how the organisation is performing against it. Try these tests:

- Run an efficiency review to ensure Production is making your products to the agreed specification. Use this template (based on Jo's performance) to understand your results. Where did your cash go? What can you improve? Have you got the right pricing model?

Widget production ingredient review

	Planned Units	Planned £	Actual Units	Actual £	Over/Under Units	Over/Under £
Volume	100	2,700	90	2,430	10	270
Chocolate		2,000		2,000		
Flapjacks		400		400		
Apples		40		40		
Profit		260		(10)	(10)	(270)

90 Units

Sales	2,430
Chocolate	2,000
Flapjacks	400
Apples	40
Net Profit	(10)

10 Units

Sales	270
Chocolate	200
Flapjacks	40
Apples	4
Net Profit	26

Performance summary

Excess ingredients	244
Lost sales	26
Lost cash	270

- Test your target. Is it still valid?

- Test your business plan. Is it still valid? What has changed?

- Review your investment and R&D programmes. Are they still valid? Test timescales and cost expectations.

- Finally, always employ a Sage who makes sense from the numbers so that everybody in the organisation understands and owns the performance of the business

Here's a great example of why you should get a 'Sage':

Creative Accounting: When Losses are Profits

A government department wanted to cut the cost of its supplies. The managers were bonused on getting these reductions. A manager in charge of toilet paper put out a tender and awarded the contract to the lowest priced bid.

The chosen supplier, not having the capability itself, in turn purchased the toilet paper from the cheapest supplier from overseas, priced in Euros.

Government employees were disappointed with the quality of the paper. Because it was so thin, they had to double up on the paper they used, therefore the department's purchases doubled.

Then the Pound/Euro exchange rate fell in value, resulting in the cost going up and the supplier losing money on the contract.

Both sides of this deal made losses, yet both managers claimed success, receiving their bonuses. How?

The Government Official calculated that because he had saved 10% on each roll sold the savings were actually greater because the Government were inexplicably using more rolls.

The supplier's manager calculated the profit from his department's figures based on the original price; exchange rate losses were the responsibility of the treasury department; So he got his bonus, and of course the salesman got his bonus long ago!

Checklist 6: Review all Fixed Costs

Fixed costs are special: once you have them, they stick to you. Taking out a lease on a property is inevitable for instance, but try to keep it flexible. Don't take out a thirty-year lease thinking you're getting a 'good price', because the reason you want that property will not exist then! You are in fact leaving an anchor for future management to drag along the floor of the ocean. Consider all these aspects of your business:

- Focus on your breakeven point. Calculate what time in the day (when in the year) you want to start making profit. The higher the fixed costs the longer it takes, and the more risk there is in your business model, so review all costs, establishing which ones can be converted into variable ones that move in line with sales.

- Consider how to outsource activities to third parties to reduce your risk of incurring costs during low sales months.

- Run an Economic Activity Review (EAR) to understand how each of the activities in your organisation is beneficial to your client. Question every activity. Why does it exist? Is there an alternative, more efficient option?

- Check what percentage of costs are fixed, then assess what the trend is as a percentage of sales. It's easy to ramp up fixed costs during a period of high activity, but install a mechanism to continually check how can they be reduced when activity reduces.

- Check your sales cycles. If they fluctuate through the year try to set your fixed costs to be low enough in the slow months, If your business is seasonal, use temporary or third party resources during busy months.

Checklist 7: The SAVE ME Template

Because business/markets/competitors/customer trends change all the time you should use the SAVE ME template as a quick check that your project/new business idea is still valid

Set a target	Is the target still valid?
Agree your plan of action	Have you adopted the most efficient plan that is currently available?
Value the new product	Revisit your market research
Explore the cost	Have the original costings remained valid?
Measure and **E**xplain results	Analyze the results and brainstorm with the team – are the numbers still valid?

Talk about scratching an itch! Jeremy Rudd addresses the very heart of the problem that every business manager and entrepreneur wrestles with: how can I make my business more profitable. Using a beautifully simple story he brings complex business principles into everyday language, enabling the reader to extract tools that they can instantly apply.

Piers Clark, Founder & Chairman Isle Group.

这是我读过的最有实用价值的经济学书！和那些枯燥乏味、冗长复杂的专业书籍相比，它不仅浅显易懂，而且书中的原理也和实际日常生活工作决策息息相关。书中的每一个要点都被解释得非常透彻，可以立刻应用到我们的日常工作中帮助我们做正确的经济决策和应对各种危机。

Juan Du, Ph.D, 10x Genomics, California

I was lucky, throughout developing my business I had the advantage of my friend nudging and guiding me through key decisions – from a two man business to a leader in the medical sector I always returned to his guidance; now that Jeremy has written this book everyone can have the same focus and guidance.

Laurence Purcell, Founder and MD, Cleanse Medical, West Midlands.

About the author

Jeremy qualified as a chartered accountant at the early age of 24 in a small practice in the north east of England, on qualifying he joined the third largest company in the UK and a leader overseas. This was an eye opener leading him to spend over thirty years in many different countries across Europe, Africa and America in countless different sectors (tanneries to paint factories, insurance companies to pathology laboratories to social housing, utilities and facilities management companies) doing what came naturally – helping businesses improve performance.

Now helping smaller businesses find their mojo again in this fast-changing world Jeremy is based in the Cotswolds in England but still travels widely (physically or by Zoom) to spread the message to entrepreneurs, business managers and owners of how to improve performance.

In the book the importance of having mentors, coaches, facilitators like Squawk is emphasised. Contact the author at squawk@4magicsteps.com to bounce off any ideas.

Four Magic Steps to Double Profit